# PHILOSOPHICAL

# PHRASES

# 111

## Metaphysical Meditations

# R.V. EVANS, MFT

The Quotes Collection (11) 111

PHILOSOPHICAL PHRASES 111

PhilosophicalPhrases111©2016R.V.Evans

United Kingdom

rvevans111@protonmail.com

R.V. Evans' Amazon Page:

R.V. Evans, MFT

# PREFACE

The Quotes Collection 111 is a series of smart sentences especially written for you. Based on different life issues, events and philosophies, these wit words of wisdom aim at uncovering old concepts, discovering new thoughts, encouraging the search for further truth, enlightening your mind, making new thought- connections, inciting a few insights or just at letting you decide whatever you want to get from them and their unique stand. You can trust The Quotes Collection 111 are always honest, true views on thoughts, feelings, facts and acts featuring fresh "words of art," original "paintings" surrounding the bright nuances of the Mind.

*Philosophy* is basically the critical evaluation of all facts of experience. By critical, I mean the careful and full examination of all the available data regarding different fields of knowledge from an objective, logical point of view. There are five main areas of philosophical study: Ethics, Epistemology and logic, Politics, Religion and Metaphysics. *Metaphysics* is the study of the "ultimate reality," that is, the examination of what transcends physical matter. Nevertheless, the present text will not address metaphysics in an academic way "per se," but rather as using the concept to describe what "goes beyond" the physical world and nature of some objects and subjects in life.

*The Philosophical Phrases* feature a one hundred and eleven metaphysical reflections and questions from different philosophical trails of thought and topics: everything from the "me" mundane moments to many mindful insights and conceptual philosophies of life. Every single one of their words has been well thought out for you to "grasp" a deep concept written in simple lines. You can trust your almighty mind to take advantage of these sets of words and sentences, to make sense of them and to accordingly applying them to your daily life to help you make the choices that are consistent with who you truly are.

Peace,

R.V. Evans, MFT

---

### JUST FOR YOU

Make sure to consult your own mind and heart before making any kind of decision in your life: the social media, internet websites and blogs, television, popular advertisement channels, strangers' reading reviews, chat rooms and any other type of mass media might be good for certain people to fulfill a specific purpose at any given time. However, they are never good enough to help you choose what is appropriate, proper, valuable, required, useful and overall right for you, for your mind, for your soul and for your life. You are the only one who has the precious responsibility, as well as the almighty right and capacity to decide for yourself what you truly need, think and want. Do not give away your right to choose who you really are for anything or for anyone!

---

R.V. Evans

# ABOUT THE AUTHOR

R. V. Evans has always been interested in the "Matters of the Mind." Ever since her younger years and even before participating in the motivational groups facilitated by her aunt Irma (a consultant Psychotherapist at the author's private school), the author envisioned Psychology as an academic path. Long before she took her first Psychology class back in college in Southern California, R. Evans had already fallen in love with such a fascinating field of study. Acknowledging everything we think, feel and do is directly dependent on and connected to what happens in this amazing abstract notion called the Mind, she decided to learn even more about it. She enrolled in college and then pursued a Master's degree in Clinical Psychology (PhD in progress). However, the passage to Psychology University was side- tracked by life's events, as well as by a number of academic and personal choices and endeavours she felt she needed to embark on first. In many ways, such a detour devised the venue for her to dive into the waters of the Mysterious Mind even deeper at a better time. Thus, knowing about mental processes and patterns of behavior helps her assist people to understand themselves and others, as well as to improve their relationships and lives, as they become more aware and in control of their reality, their motivations and their choices.

Bright choices, awareness, motivation and a true feeling of freedom are the ultimate tools for building a satisfying emotional life. This truth became even more evident through countless academic and clinical hours and experiences. R. Evans has become a prolific Psychological Therapist, able to recognize, address and provide the right professional insight and information, always observing respect, empathy, honesty, confidentiality and sensible timing on each intervention. Knowing well the "What to say, When to say it, Who to say it and How to say it (©3WH)", is a well-developed therapeutic skill, a "trademark" in R. V. Evans counselling style. More importantly, finding the way to interpret the relationship individuals have with their own selves and experiences, and being aware of the meaning they give to them, is key in helping them to connect with themselves in a more genuine, responsible manner, so they are able to make better decisions in their everyday life. This is possible through the use of the appropriate therapeutic blended approach: Humanistic Existential therapy and other therapeutic modalities.

By applying the Humanistic Existential approach to therapy blended with other modalities (eclectic therapy) combined with integrity, respect, empathy and clear communication, R. V. Evans can make "close contact" with her client's fascinating trail of thought. In this way, she uncovers the mind's fantastic functions, its components, manifestations (emotions and behaviors) and its crucial connections, as well as the implications in the client's life in the "material world" of overt and covert behavior in the here and now, to establish its impact on a wide range of moments and situations.

R. V. Evans believes the best and only way to lead a life worth living is by being your true self. Expressing the contents of your soul and mind in an authentic manner is essential to exist as a free thinking being. Freedom brings comfort. Comfort brings what you perceive as satisfaction. And, satisfaction gives you the motivational attitude you need to give yourself and others all the best you deserve. This alone, may well be a justifiable life purpose. Therefore, is imperative for you to know the exact nature of your mind and learn to identify which makes you express your inner truth in the most genuine, legitimate way. R. V. Evans will provide you with as many choices as you need to make the right decision work for you to succeed in seeing your true self, as well as in expressing yourself every day, as you acknowledge and appreciate the most important person in your world: You... and then, some more. Just as R. V. Evans would say: "Enjoy the best way to be: Your True Self."

M. Bulman

United Kingdom

# CONTENT

Herein you will find *One Hundred and Eleven* insightful Philosophical Phrases, metaphysical thoughts and reflections for you to explore and evaluate as you build and shape your own thought- transformations.

Happy Insights!

R.V. Evans, MFT

"A bridge between reality and virtuality

connects all concepts to their true actuality."

My Thought- Transformation:

"All concrete objects are potentially invisible

in the physical and abstract planes of the admissible."

My Thought- Transformation:

"The nature of thoughts originates as a causal- effect

interpretation of the subconscious mind."

My Thought- Transformation:

"Virtual and Ultimate realities transcend

the material manifestation of their intention and aim."

My Thought- Transformation:

"If it cannot be experienced, it cannot be known,

but knowing an un-experienced experience

is within the realms of knowledge."

My Thought- Transformation:

"Mind- Philosophy **determines which** thoughts

are inherently conceived inside of the mind."

My Thought- Transformation:

"Between 'before physics' and 'after physics'

there is a whole world of innate possibilities."

My Thought- Transformation:

"Everything is true and everything is false;

potentialities make possible to consider each cause."

My Thought- Transformation:

"The essential matter of reality is space-less

and timeless, as it is infinite and boundless."

My Thought- Transformation:

"Which thoughts are purely fabricated outside

the concrete existence of facts?"

My Thought- Transformation:

"Existence is the content of thought;

thought is the principle of Being."

My Thought- Transformation:

"Reality is in a constant state of flux:

evolution is motionless moving moments of static awareness."

My Thought- Transformation:

"The main source of mindful motion is emotion:

only love or hate promote movement and change."

My Thought- Transformation:

"Reason is the unchanging modifying cause

of the concepts of order, beauty, purpose and law."

My Thought- Transformation:

"Innumerable atoms fill infinite space

causing a number of changes in the entire universe."

My Thought- Transformation:

"Ultimate reality is one in number and kind

just and only in the here and now."

My Thought- Transformation:

"The infinite possesses an infinite array

of finite features expressed in infinite ways."

My Thought- Transformation:

"Existence **occupies** physical **and** non- physical **space.**"

My Thought- Transformation:

- 19 -

"The more the mind believes the fruition of a wish

is already taking place, the more it is surely already

materializing in the reality- plane of space."

My Thought- Transformation:

"The virtual value of an object or subject

is actually set by the exclusivity of its possession."

My Thought- Transformation:

"Mind is the manifestation of matter

as matter is manifested by the mind."

My Thought- Transformation:

"Space, mass and motion are primary qualities of objects;

color, sound and taste are psychological secondary traits.

My Thought- Transformation:

"The relationship, connection and order of all concepts are equivalent

to the order, connection and relationship of all subjects and events."

My Thought- Transformation:

"Ultimate reality is like water: a gaseous, solid and liquid matter."

My Thought- Transformation:

"The metaphysically genuine matter of the mind

is its most realistic, idealist characteristic and flaw."

My Thought- Transformation:

"Atoms are governed by eternal, uncaused, permanently

dynamic and indestructible codes of behavior."

My Thought- Transformation:

"Are reality comforting conceptions a mere description

of the contents of content, indolent minds?"

My Thought- Transformation:

"Mathematical concepts are peculiar creations which can never be materially, nor essentially modified by change, space or time.

My Thought- Transformation:

"The Supreme Value in the Universe is something unchangeable, everlasting, harmonious, creative and morally transcendent."

My Thought- Transformation:

"What is true for one individual is only true for all individuals

if the notion abides to the laws of objectivity"

My Thought- Transformation:

"Human perception reveals a relative, unnatural reality;

Human reason detects the absolute reality of Nature."

My Thought- Transformation:

"Numbers are the man- made virtual, ultimate reality

used to perpetuate the permanence and imperishable immutability

of universally acclaimed valid values."

My Thought- Transformation:

"The principles of tangible reality only exist

in the metaphysical world of abstract thought."

My Thought- Transformation:

"What lacks matter must be understood

to give it substance, understanding and mood."

My Thought- Transformation:

"An essence inherent in presence has the potential

to be fully actualized through its aimed existence."

My Thought- Transformation:

"The conception and inception of natural notions

are contingent on their practical application

as well as on their mind- realization."

My Thought- Transformation:

"The Mind's highest virtue is to Know... full stop."

My Thought- Transformation:

"The Ultimate Matter differs from the Matrix in nature:

independence, essence and purpose make up its final function."

My Thought- Transformation:

"Idiosyncratic design determines the behavior,

connection and interaction of all notions on Earth and beyond."

My Thought- Transformation:

"The Mind- Body is not a philosophical problem:

harmless harmony, complying complicity, interacting attraction

and aim affinity make of this partnership a logical probability."

My Thought- Transformation:

"Do all notions - substantial or abstract - possess

an inherent 'heart', soul, psyche or mind?"

My Thought- Transformation:

"Is the Truth a dichotomy comprising both,

the truths of Reason and truths of Fact?

If so, how can we blend them to reconcile them at last?

My Thought- Transformation:

"The Truths of Reason are free and follow the principles of logic;

these truths are eternal, structured and innately understood."

My Thought- Transformation:

"The truths of Fact are contingent: they emerge

from phenomenological, perceived experience."

My Thought- Transformation:

"Sufficient Reason may be just the first step

to understand all notions and conditions."

My Thought- Transformation:

"There is no need for evil to justify intelligence and freedom:

both, reason and choice, are inherently creative forces in the world."

My Thought- Transformation:

"At birth, the human mind is a 'tabula rasa' (blank tablet);

perception and interpretation of experience

are the bright ink used to write the book of life."

My Thought- Transformation:

"Knowledge is only possible through the processing

of experiences in the form of insightful reasoning."

My Thought- Transformation:

- 49 -

"Discerning between sensations and interpretations

is the key to truth- experience and reality appreciation."

My Thought- Transformation:

"Ontological **Reality** is the Mother **of all** realities."

My Thought- Transformation:

- 51 -

"Unobserved gravity is like oxygen:

it cannot be seen, nevertheless, it is sensed and perceived

by the unperceivable entities of the vast reality."

My Thought- Transformation:

"The drive of self-preservation is a metaphysical reality:

an irrational will to live is in itself an infinite motivational deed."

My Thought- Transformation:

"All material and immaterial worlds

are just objects in relation to subject perception: ideas."

My Thought- Transformation:

"Strong determination to achieve immortality and a healthy life

is incoherent if it disregards what is intelligent, decent and wise."

My Thought- Transformation:

"The fundamental nature of the universe can only be unveiled

by understanding the basis, dynamics and essence

of the relationship between reality and appearance."

My Thought- Transformation:

- 56 -

"Explaining the Being is as possible as probabilities of all kinds are:

the ultimate entity is, and always will be, the real substance of the mind."

My Thought- Transformation:

"The Being exists in an empty space, a meaningless portion

of Universal Reality filled up with a billion of purposeful notions."

My Thought- Transformation:

"Ultimate reality is unique, unborn, everlasting, but limited."

My Thought- Transformation:

"The nature of metaphysical reality is *Becoming*."

My Thought- Transformation:

"Reality is a process: motion is the method and action of all things."

My Thought- Transformation:

"The Being's inborn properties have natural Ebbs and flows."

My Thought- Transformation:

- 62 -

"Identity and behavior are inseparable parts of the Being's core

and an inherent component of its present and future nature."

My Thought- Transformation:

"The primordial motivational force for change of any subject

in nature resides in its power for adaptive expression."

My Thought- Transformation:

"Every object in nature is composed of several unique elements,

differing from each other in their dominant structural idiosyncrasies."

My Thought- Transformation:

"The indubitability of the mind is its 'trait of proof.'

Its proof is inherent to the existence of its disproof."

My Thought- Transformation:

"Everything and everyone is created for an ultimate,

unique, particular and practical purpose."

My Thought- Transformation:

"The value of virtue consists in doing the right thing, at the right time, in the right manner: *right* meaning useful, decent and everlasting."

My Thought- Transformation:

"Avoidance of pain is in itself an ultimate life purpose."

My Thought- Transformation:

"Self- gratification **and** sensual pleasures **are** inherent rights

of the Being, **as long as they abide to the** laws **of decency**

**and of self and communal** well- being."

My Thought- Transformation:

"Fear of death is needless: when we are alive, there is no death and when we die, that is all it is. Fear is not real, not even as an emotion. It is just a superfluous habit about a popular notion.

My Thought- Transformation:

"'Peace of Mind' is of superb, perpetual worth as long

as you give 'peace' the meaning your mind longs for."

My Thought- Transformation:

"Self- control and self- mastery may be the perfect

Self- transcendence tools as long as they express

the ultimate true aim of the soul."

My Thought- Transformation:

"The ultimate meaning of meaning is only given

by the holder of its aim and purpose."

My Thought- Transformation:

"Pleasure is of one quality only: physical.

Even spiritual pleasure is material in its sensual nature."

My Thought- Transformation:

"Satisfaction of the senses differs only quantitatively: their satiation

may just vary in their intensity, capacity and duration."

My Thought- Transformation:

"The ultimate concept of Ethics is basically based on the notion

of 'good will,' only if 'good' means 'communal benefit,'

and 'will,' means 'determined obligation'."

My Thought- Transformation:

"The ultimate value of Justice resides in its primitive pursue

and its mechanical methods to attain its primordial purpose: balance.

My Thought- Transformation:

"The abstract reality of Matter goes beyond

the completion of its essential actualization."

My Thought- Transformation:

"The world of existence can only be realized by the acceptance

of the presence of the permanent blend of matter and profile."

My Thought- Transformation:

"The process of reality transmutation takes place in the mind

as potential reality transpires from essence to actual presence."

My Thought- Transformation:

"*Nothingness,* **as the** extinction **of all human** impulses,

annihilates **human** creative **purpose for** breathing **and** transcending."

My Thought- Transformation:

"The ultimate extent of space is limited as it is infinite."

My Thought- Transformation:

"*Logos*, the logic of the universe, as the uniform, essential,

naturally cognizant law is the only permanent reality code."

My Thought- Transformation:

"Knowledge can only be attained by the detached judgement of the facts, components and pacts that reign and condition its applied definition."

My Thought- Transformation:

"The worlds of the known and the knowable

fuse in the universe of all: The Ideas World.

My Thought- Transformation:

"The unfolding of reality is affected in the way

it establishes its effect, its effort and its aim."

My Thought- Transformation:

"The law of preservation should only apply

to what is worth preserving."

My Thought- Transformation:

"The indiscriminate and continual satiation of essential indulgence may disappear it, dilute it or even cause it to convert it into pain."

My Thought- Transformation:

"Beyond the value of adaptation and acceptance, is the actualization

of acknowledging what does not have modification."

My Thought- Transformation:

"Even ephemerous objects can hold an eternal control

over the mind through values, beliefs, will and wants."

My Thought- Transformation:

"Perpetual peace can be achieved through the awareness

and understanding of the true nature of all objects."

My Thought- Transformation:

"Loss is relative: learning to live with unavoidable pain

is what makes life and grief easy to celebrate."

My Thought- Transformation:

"If what cannot be thought cannot exist,

How to explain what has no concept

in the realm of the unknown?"

My Thought- Transformation:

"Absolutely, energy is never created;

Relatively, energy never perishes."

My Thought- Transformation:

"Reality possess relative existence only to the eyes of the beholder."

My Thought- Transformation:

"The nature of human nature is unnatural in its essential nature."

My Thought- Transformation:

"Permanence, immutability, harmony, beauty and validity

in eternity are some of the values of imperishable numerology."

My Thought- Transformation:

"Atoms only mutate in order of organization:

true transformation occurs

at the core of their usefulness and function."

My Thought- Transformation:

"Any notion beyond the bounds of experience should be acknowledged,

as long as understanding, knowledge and wisdom

can be extracted from its empirical envision."

My Thought- Transformation:

- 101 -

"The mind, nature and reality spread and progress

by means of distinctive dialectic encounters."

My Thought- Transformation:

"Two opposite sides collide producing an irremediable reconciliation by the imminent emerging novelty of possibilities and anticipation."

My Thought- Transformation:

"In subjects, will manifests as instincts and vanity;

in objects, will manifests as physical forces, like gravity."

My Thought- Transformation:

"Will is the real inner nature of the Being

and it ultimately manifests as a constant, creative notion for fruition."

My Thought- Transformation:

"The most transcendental form of behavior is compassion:

through empathic actions, humanity celebrates and perpetuates

the core values of human existence, its worth and its value."

My Thought- Transformation:

"Transcendental reality serves humanity

as great ideas and useful ideals of reason."

My Thought- Transformation:

"Awareness of reality and its contents, including absent subjects,

is the realization of the purpose of human existence and co- existence."

My Thought- Transformation:

"Human isolation is an impossibility:

the realms of necessity establish relationships

and relatedness as an inherent function of human nature."

My Thought- Transformation:

"The mind is rational and true

in nature, and the Truth is absolute of the mind."

My Thought- Transformation:

"At the core of the nature of Logic, we admit

that Reality ought to be understood rather than just perceived."

My Thought- Transformation:

"The ultimate expression of wisdom

is eliminating self- absorbed behavior."

My Thought- Transformation:

THANK YOU FOR READING

See you in my next book!

R. V. Evans' Amazon Page:

R.V. Evans, MFT

rvevans111@protonmail.com

Printed in Great Britain
by Amazon

32940519R00066